BUILDING LEADERSHIP CHARACTER

COACH'S EDITION: BOOK ONE

DEDICATION

This book is dedicated to all the coaches that sacrifice their time and talents to serve the Lord by leading their athletes for the glory of God!

Kingdom Sports: Coach's Edition: Book One

Gordon Thiessen, Rod Handley, Wes Neal, Ron Brown and Josh Thiessen

ISBN 978-1-938254-91-8

Cross Training Publishing
15418 Weir Street #177
Omaha, NE 68137
(308) 293-3891
www.crosstrainingpublishing.com
www.kingdomsports.online

Copyright © 2019 by Cross Training Publishing

All rights reserved. No part of this book may be reproduced without written permission from the publisher, except by a reviewer who may quote brief passages in a review; nor may any part of this book be reproduced, stored in a retrieval system or transmitted in any form or other without written permission from the publisher.

This book is manufactured in the United States of America.

Library of Congress Cataloging in Publication Data in Progress.

START HERE!

First, begin by choosing the study that best fits your time frame. You can choose between Section One (45 minutes) and Section Two (30 minutes). If you don't choose Section One, you might consider having your group read the additional material that is provided as an assignment during the week. You should also consider assigning the Bible reading plan and video lesson.

Second, make sure you have enough books for everyone in your study, and download the videos for each lesson at www.kingdomsports.online. .

It's that simple! Once you finish your study, you can continue this character series for coaches with Book 2 and Book 3. There is also an athlete's study series available as well. You can also find many other valuable resources at www.crosstrainingpublishing.com.

The Gospel

According to the Bible, God designed each of us to reflect the moral nature of God Himself. For that reason, the character traits taught in this book are directly related to the character of God.

The authors have tried not to simply teach moral lessons and put teaching character traits ahead of the main thing, which is the Gospel: God sent His Son to the cross to bear His wrath for sinners like you and me. Don't allow this or any other study on character to become just good advice rather than good news.

In order to understand the Gospel, we need to understand the facts behind it. Below are the facts I share about God whenever I have the chance to talk about the Gospel.

GOSPEL FACTS

That the one and only one God, who is holy, made us in His image to know Him. However, we have sinned and cut ourselves off from Him. Because of God's love for us, God became a man in Jesus, lived a perfect life, and died on the cross. He fulfilled the law Himself by taking on the punishment we deserved for the sins of all those who ever turn and trust Him. He rose again from the dead, showing that God accepted Christ's sacrifice and that God's wrath against us had been exhausted. Now, God calls us to repent of our sins and trust in Christ; we are born again into a new life, an eternal life with God.

Let me remind you that the Gospel is more than a door we walk through to become a Christian. The Gospel is not only for the lost but also for the found. The cross and its meaning aren't something that we ever master. David Prior said, "We never move on from the cross, only to a more profound understanding of the cross."

I hope you will find this book both interesting and helpful to your Christian life. May you always see Christ's character and desire to see it reproduced in your own life, and may pursuing Godly character produce in you a more profound understanding of the cross. — The Publisher, Gordon Thiessen

Contents

Section One • 45 minutes

Lesson 1   *A Leader is Loyal* 11
            John 21:15-19

Lesson 2   *A Leader is a Servant-Leader* 15
            Matthew 20:20-28

Lesson 3   *A Leader Guards Their Heart* 19
            Matthew 6:19-24

Lesson 4   *A Leader Depends on God* 23
            Matthew 6:25-30

Lesson 5   *A Leader Sacrifices for Others* 27
            Romans 5:6-11

Lesson 6   *A Leader is Confident* 31
            Romans 8:28-30

Lesson 7   *A Leader is Truthful* 35
            Ephesians 4:17-25

Lesson 8   *A Leader is Poised* 39
            Luke 20:1-8

Lesson 9   *A Leader is Purposeful* 43
            John 12:36-43

Lesson 10   *A Leader is Self-Controlled* 47
            1 Corinthians 10:6-13

Lesson 11   *A Leader is Energetic* 51
            Philippians 4:10-19

Lesson 12   *A Leader is Determined* 55
            Philippians 3:12-16

Section Two • 30 minutes

Lesson 1   *A Leader is Loyal* 61
            John 21:15-19

Lesson 2   *A Leader is a Servant-Leader* 63
            Matthew 20:20-28

Lesson 3   *A Leader Guards Their Heart* 65
            Matthew 6:19-24

Lesson 4   *A Leader Depends on God* 67
            Matthew 6:25-30

Lesson 5   *A Leader Sacrifices for Others* 69
            Romans 5:6-11

Lesson 6	*A Leader is Confident*	71
	Romans 8:28-30	
Lesson 7	*A Leader is Truthful*	73
	phesians 4:17-25	
Lesson 8	*A Leader is Poised*	75
	Luke 20:1-8	
Lesson 9	*A Leader is Purposeful*	77
	John 12:36-43	
Lesson 10	*A Leader is Self-Controlled*	79
	1 Corinthians 10:6-13	
Lesson 11	*A Leader is Energetic*	81
	Philippians 4:10-19	
Lesson 12	*A Leader is Determined*	83
	Philippians 3:12-16	

AUTHORS

GORDON THIESSEN is a publisher, author, photographer and speaker. He has published more than one hundred books on sports and competition. He is the author of "Cross Training Workout," "Headline Sports Devotions," "Beyond the Headlines" and two new books "Lessons from Nebraska Football" and "Peak Performance." He served with the Nebraska Fellowship of Christian Athletes for 28 years before co-founding Kingdom Sports @ www.kingdomsports.online.

ROD HANDLEY is the former Chief Operating Officer & Chief Financial Officer for the Fellowship of Christian Athletes (FCA). He is currently the Founder and President of Character That Counts, a ministry founded in July 2000. He is a popular retreat and banquet speaker with men's and women's groups, singles and married. Rod has published nineteen books, including, "Character Counts—Who's Counting Yours?" which details how to begin the process of being accountable to one another. Rod and his wife Janna live in Lee's Summit, MO, and they have four children.

RON BROWN was born in New York City and raised in Massachusetts. Ron was an assistant coach for the Nebraska Cornhusker football team for 24 years before returning as the Director of Player Development for the football team. Ron co-founded Kingdom Sports. He and his wife Molvina live in Lincoln with their two daughters, Sojourner and Bronwyn.

JOSH THIESSEN is a graduate of The Master's Seminary. From 2007-2009 Josh served as a pastoral assistant at Grace Community Church in Los Angeles, CA while finishing his M.Div and Th.M. Currently he serves as the pastor at Providence Bible Church in Omaha.

SECTION ONE

BUILDING LEADERSHIP CHARACTER
COACH'S EDITION
45 MINUTES

---- LESSON 1 ----

A LEADER IS LOYAL

"Many a man proclaims his own loyalty, but who can find a trustworthy man?"

Proverbs 20:6

When Tom Osborne retired, more than 700 players and coaches who had been part of the Nebraska football program attended his retirement banquet. Their devotion and loyalty toward the man they simply called "Coach" was clearly in response to the admiration and loyalty instilled in them. During his career, the average tenure for Osborne's assistant coaches was 14 years, compared to three years at other schools. He was well known for standing behind his players and remaining loyal to them even when they got into trouble. Most famously, he continued to support Lawrence Phillips when most coaches would have given up on him. Phillips was the troubled running back who later had a brief career in the NFL. Speaking of Phillips, he said, "My faith has led me to believe that no person is exempt from the pull of God or beyond redemption, including Lawrence. One of the last times I saw Lawrence I gave him a New Testament and explained that the only solution I saw would involve a spiritual commitment."

1. What stands out to you in Coach Osborne's statement?

2. What was the motivation for Coach Osborne's handling of Lawrence Phillips? What is it about his faith that would compel Osborne to remain loyal to Phillips?

WARM UP

What exactly is loyalty? Loyalty is faithfulness toward a person or an ideal. Loyalty is a virtue often overlooked in our culture today. With so many corrupt leaders taking advantage of their positions of power, many think this important virtue is a weakness rather than a strength. But Scripture regards this quality as important for any leader.

In a real sense, "we are all each other's bodyguard." Loyalty involves protecting those around us. We believe in and want the best for each other. We have a stake in the life of each person. We value one other. We strengthen and inspire each other.

Coaches look for loyalty in those they serve. Jesus Christ required loyalty from His disciples and he also requires it from Christians today challenging us to take up our crosses daily (Luke 9:23).

1. Which sports teams did you grow up following? Are you still loyal to them? Why or why not?

2. Discuss the role of loyalty on good teams.

3. Coach John Wooden said loyalty was a key factor in the foundation for his Pyramid of Success. The main ingredient in stardom, he told his players, "is the rest of the team." When teaching on loyalty, he taught "Be true to yourself. Be true to those you lead." Discuss these statements by Coach Wooden.

4. What are some different reasons people might remain loyal to their organization or leader?

5. Read Proverbs 20:6, "Who can find a faithful man?" Is it difficult to find loyal athletes today? Why or why not?

WORKOUT

JOHN 21:15-19

When they had finished breakfast, Jesus said to Simon Peter, "Simon, son of John, do you love me more than these?" He said to him, "Yes, Lord; you know that I love you." He said to him, "Feed my lambs." He said to him a second time, "Simon, son of John, do you love me?" He said to him, "Yes, Lord; you know that I love you." He said to him, "Tend my sheep." He said to him the third time, "Simon, son of John, do you love me?" Peter was grieved because he said to him the third time, "Do you love me?" and he said to him, "Lord, you know everything; you know that I love you." Jesus said to him, "Feed my sheep. Truly, truly, I say to you, when you were young, you used to dress yourself and walk wherever you wanted, but when you are old, you will stretch out your hands, and another will dress you and carry you where you do not want to go." And after saying this he said to him, "Follow me."

CONTEXT

This exchange between Peter and Jesus occurred after the crucifixion and resurrection and is known as the restoration of Peter. Prior to the death of Christ, Peter had proclaimed his loyalty to Jesus no matter the cost—even if all the others fell away, Peter swore that he would remain! And yet just a short time later Peter denied that he even knew who Jesus was, not once but three times! The Lord addressed Peter by his original name (Simon), as if he had forfeited the strength of his new name Peter, the rock, through denying Christ.

EXPLORE THE MEANING

1. What stands out to you in this passage?
2. Explain how Peter must have felt when he was questioned for the third time? Can you relate to this as a coach?

MAN'S WAY OR GOD'S WAY?

When adversity strikes, man-centered loyalty fails just as Peter's pledge did, but biblical loyalty is compelled by love and includes a commitment to God. It's built on the foundation of Jesus' demonstration of His loyal love for us, which in turn produces a love response of loyalty back to Him and those around us.

GOING DEEPER

1. What's the difference between how man *proclaims* loyalty and a truly trustworthy man (Proverbs 20:6)?

2. Could you explain to someone where your greatest loyalty lies and why? How does your response compare to the Gospel message Christ presents?

3. As you think about Osborne's reason for supporting his player, how did the Gospel influence what he did?

COACHING GOD'S WAY

Jesus demonstrated loyalty toward Peter even when he failed to follow Him. Peter probably didn't deserve a second chance. However, Jesus was more than willing to restore his relationship with Him. This example of Jesus toward Peter encourages me to forgive my players when they have failed. I often say to a player that blows it, "That's not you." While they need to be corrected, I want them to know I haven't given up on them. I can see beyond their failure, just as Jesus did with Peter. It's much easier for me to have this attitude when I remind myself how the Lord has forgiven my sins.

ASSIGNMENT
- Bible reading: John chapters 1-2.
  Watch Lesson #1 @ www.kingdomsports.online

---- LESSON 2 ----

A LEADER IS A SERVANT-LEADER

"For even the Son of Man came not to be served but to serve, and to give his life as a ransom for many."

Mark 10:45

Over the years, the late Kay Yow (formerly of North Carolina State) and current Nevada Head Coach Jane Albright developed a close friendship. In *Leader of the Pack: The Legacy of Legendary Coach Kay Yow*, Albright recalls when Yow joined her family for one of many Christmas dinners. "On Christmas 2006, when Kay was right in the middle of her fight with cancer, we were all scared she would not be able to come, but late that day she arrived, once again bearing special stories and gifts. Kay rarely talked about herself, but this Christmas she spoke of her battle with cancer and the hundreds of letters she had received from people who had prayed for her and wanted to encourage her. She explained that she didn't have the energy to respond to each letter. I quickly told her that all of these people, most of whom didn't know her personally, did not expect an answer to their words. 'But I at least want to answer the young people's letters,' she said. 'You know, letter writing is a dying thing now and I want to encourage them to write more of them.' Only Kay Yow would take something meant just for her and turn it back to the giver."

1. Describe a servant-coach in your own words.
2. What impact do servant-leaders have on your team?

WARM UP

A coach or a team leader has to count the cost of the position, for the price of leadership is sacrificial servanthood. It requires laying down your life for the people you are leading. All personal glory must be set aside to serve your team.

Jesus knew that love and leadership would lead to sacrifice. His love led Him to die in our place. That's REAL sacrifice! Christ-like servant-leadership means considering the needs of your staff and team before your own, seeking their good, encouraging their growth, and relationship with God. It means trying to treat others the way God has treated us. Christ-like servant leaders employ gentle guidance rather than barking orders and ultimatums. They don't dictate or demand but recognize that before God, they themselves are but servants who are simply doing their duty (Luke 17:10).

As a coach, give careful consideration to your own life. Is your life one that others would choose to imitate? Are you willing to lay down your life for your staff and team? David Roper said this about serving others: "Whatever our position of leadership, we will never lose if we lose ourselves for others. Service that cares for others is the basis of true greatness." Today, choose to be a servant-leader.

1. Do you consider yourself a servant-leader? Why or why not?

2. How can you become a Christ-like coach with your staff and team?

3. What sacrifice(s) will you have to make to become a better servant-leader?

4. How does Jesus' sacrifice compare to the sacrifices you make?

WORKOUT

MATTHEW 20:20-28

Then the mother of the sons of Zebedee came up to him with her sons, and kneeling before him she asked him for something. And he said to her, "What do you want?" She said to him, "Say that these two sons of mine are to sit, one at your right hand and one at your left, in your kingdom." Jesus answered, "You do not know what you are asking. Are you able to drink the cup that I am to drink?" They said to him, "We are able." He said to them, "You will drink my cup, but to sit at my right hand and at my left is not mine to grant, but it is for those for whom it has been prepared by my Father." And when the ten heard it, they were indignant at the two brothers. But Jesus called them to him and said, "You know that the rulers of the Gentiles lord it over them, and their great ones exercise authority over them. It shall not be so among you. But whoever would be great among you must be your servant, and whoever would be first among you must be your slave, even as the Son of Man came not to be served but to serve, and to give his life as a ransom for many."

CONTEXT

This passage teaches both the right and wrong reasons for desiring leadership. James and John recruited their mother to present their proud and self-seeking request to Jesus. Since their mother was the sister of Jesus' mother, they very likely thought her appeal would influence Jesus' response. Even today, it's not uncommon for people to seek positions of leadership for reasons other than being the best qualified person for the job. The cup is an Old Testament symbol. Jesus is asking the disciples if they are ready to suffer to the degree that He was, to drink the whole cup? This is Jesus' way of teaching that leadership involves suffering. There is a price to be paid for being a leader.

EXPLORE THE MEANING

1. What stands out to you in this passage?
2. Former NFL coach Mike Holmgren went 0-24 when he began his coaching career in high school. What can this type of hardship teach us about servant-leadership?

MAN'S WAY OR GOD'S WAY?

In this passage of Scripture, the Lord teaches the disciples that the style of leadership for believers should be different than that of non-believers. The non-believing Gentile leaders dominated in a dictatorial style, using whatever means necessary to control their followers. This style of leadership is still common today among many coaches. However, true spiritual leadership means loving service to one another. The real leader is a coach who serves, not a coach who demands to be served.

GOING DEEPER

1. Jesus said, "...to give His life a ransom for many (v. 28). The word translated "for" means "in the place of." This verse shows the substitutionary nature of Christ's sacrifice. Further, a "ransom" is a price paid to redeem a slave. How does this apply to coaching?

COACHING GOD'S WAY

As a young coach, I was greatly impressed by watching Raymond Berry demonstrate servant-leadership on the New England Patriots team. He would often draw up scout cards or other duties normally relegated to managers. He was showing his players servant-leadership without saying a single word. I have tried my best to learn from his example.

ASSIGNMENT

- Bible reading: John chapters 3-4.
  Watch Lesson #2 @ www.kingdomsports.online

---- LESSON 3 ----

A LEADER GUARDS THEIR HEART

"Keep your heart with all vigilance, for from it flow the springs of life"

Proverbs 4:23

Ohio State football's memorabilia-for-cash and tattoos scandal forced coach Jim Tressel to resign following a stellar career that included an overall record of 94–22. He failed to report information about players involved with the incident. Jason Wright a former NFL veteran, had this to say about Coach Tressel. "I believe Jim Tressel loves God. I believe he has faith that Jesus is the Son of God and the Savior of the world. I also believe that he has a real personal relationship with the one true God. During my time playing for the Cleveland Browns, I was repeatedly told of the stellar job he did representing the faith at churches, parachurch fundraisers, and other Christian gatherings. I've heard equally positive reports from his former players. And I don't think he was faking." While some fans might debate Wright's assessment, this is a reminder to all coaches that if something like this can happen to Jim Tressel, it can happen to any coach who fails to guard his heart.

1. While we can't know for sure Coach Tressel's motivation in failing to report the player violations, we do know it cost him his job. What are some temptations coaches face?
2. What makes it so difficult for coaches or athletes to admit their faults?

WARM UP

Proverbs 4:23 says, "Above all else guard your heart for from it flows the wellsprings of life." Another translation says it this way, "From your heart flows everything." When Scripture speaks of the heart, it's speaking of your thought life, the core of your soul, where your thoughts operate. Jerry Bridges said, "The word heart in Scripture is used in various ways. The MIND as it reasons, discerns and judges; the EMOTIONS as they like or dislike; the CONSCIENCE as it determines and warns and the WILL as it chooses or refuses—are all together called the heart."

The subject of the heart is addressed in the Bible more than any other topic—more than works or service, more than belief or obedience, more than money, and even more than worship. Proverbs 21:2 says, "All a man's ways seem right to him, but the Lord weighs the heart." John MacArthur states, "The single most important battlefield in the struggle for integrity is your own mind or heart. That's where everything will actually be won or lost. And if you lose there, you have already ruined your character."

One of the greatest threats to the heart is idolatry. Ken Sande says, "An idol is not simply a statue of wood, stone, or metal; it is anything we love and pursue in place of God, and can also be referred to as a 'false god' or a 'functional god.' In biblical terms, an idol is something other than God that we set our hearts on, that motivates us, that masters or rules us, or that we serve."

1. How is idolatry a problem in coaching and sports?

2. How do the following statements relate to coaching?

    "The evil in our desire typically does not lie in what we want, but that we want it too much." —John Calvin
    "But each one is tempted when, by his own evil desire, he is dragged away and enticed." James 1:14

WORKOUT

MATTHEW 6:19-24

Do not lay up for yourselves treasures upon earth, where moth and rust destroy, and where thieves break in and steal. But lay up for yourselves treasures in heaven, where neither moth nor rust destroys, and where thieves do not break in or steal; for where your treasure is, there will your heart be also. The lamp of the body is the eye; if therefore your eye is clear, your whole body will be full of light. But if your eye is bad, your whole body will be full of darkness. If therefore the light that is in you is darkness, how great is the darkness! No one can serve two masters; for either he will hate the one and love the other, or he will hold to one and despise the other. You cannot serve God and mammon.

CONTEXT

It has been said that the Bible views the heart as the human mission control center. It is out of the heart that man operates. To the authors of the Bible, the heart was much more than an organ pumping blood or the emotionally driven concept that we have today. It involved all of oneself. Here Jesus is drilling down to what really matters by asking the most important question, "Who do you serve?" And this question has eternal consequences.

EXPLORE THE MEANING

1. What stands out to you in this passage?

2. Why does Jesus link one's desires to their pocketbook?

3. What matters most to coaches? How does that impact their lives?

MAN'S WAY OR GOD'S WAY?

The relationship in this passage is that of a slave to a master. A slave cannot be owned by two people. However, many coaches spend their entire careers serving several masters. Even for the Christian coach this is a challenge. Scripture doesn't teach that a believer won't be tempted by idolatry and sin. How each person spends his time, talents and treasures, etc. will show who he is truly owned by. If you truly belong to Jesus, then you will guard your heart so that it seeks His glory above all things. So the question remains, are you storing up treasure in heaven or collecting wood, hay and stubble?

GOING DEEPER

1. What treasures might coaches store up for themselves?
2. What motivates you? How do you spend your time?

COACHING GOD'S WAY

One of my responsibilities as a running back coach is to make sure my players properly protect the quarterback on pass protection. Leaving the quarterback unguarded is disastrous. It's no different when it comes to leaving our own hearts unprotected. I'm going to guard my heart with everything I have. Here are just a few ways to guard your heart.

1. Read the Bible every day.
2. Meditate on the Word.
3. Scripture memory.
4. Commune with God in prayer.
5. Be careful what you look at.
6. Be careful what you listen to.

ASSIGNMENT

- Bible reading: John chapter 5.
  Watch Lesson #3 @ www.kingdomsports.online

LESSON 4

A LEADER DEPENDS ON GOD

"It does not, therefore, depend on man's desire or effort, but on God's mercy."

Romans 9:16

"Football is a profession that is judged by performance and results," says Tony Dungy, former head coach of the Indianapolis Colts. "However, those things come and go so quickly that as a coach, I had to depend on something more." Tony Dungy is a devout Christian who depends on God to strive for excellence. In his own words, what follows is his explanation of the source of his strength and character.

"When I went to the Steelers in 1977, there was a group of guys who were different than any I had ever been around—guys like Donnie Shell, Mel Blount, Jon Kolb and Larry Brown. They were very focused players who loved football and Jesus. As I watched them, I sensed something very unique, and I realized it was their relationship with Jesus Christ that made them different. Their decisions were based on Christ, because they believed He has the answers for everything. They helped me straighten out my priorities."

1. How are coaches and their families affected by other's judgment of performance and results?
2. Name a few coaches who have left coaching because the profession is so stressful and demanding,

WARM UP

To depend on God means that you have faith, but faith is more than saying "I believe." To believe in what you see requires no faith. However, believing in something you cannot see is genuine faith. Faith is a willingness to act upon your belief.

Hebrews 11 is often called the "Hall of Faith." It has numerous examples of men and women who took God at His Word and depended on Him for the results. One example of this is Enoch, described in Genesis 5:24 as a man "who walked with God." His walk, based on faith, had remarkable results, as noted in Hebrews 11:5. Enoch pleased God by faith. True faith extends beyond just "intellectual faith" by inviting us to be obedient. Obedience means completely depending upon God.

Faith is trusting in God's providence and care. Faith is an attitude that declares, "I don't know what God is doing, but I believe that whatever it is, it's His best for my life." A coach who has faith does not need all the answers because he has the presence and love of Christ as his hope. Scripture teaches that the object of faith is Christ Himself, not a creed or a promise (John 3:16). Faith therefore involves personal commitment to Christ (2 Cor. 5:15).

1. The key to understanding faith lies not in faith itself but in the OBJECT of faith. Do you agree or disagree with this statement? Explain your answer.

2. How would you describe your own faith in Jesus Christ?

3. How well do you respond when life situations don't go like you've planned? What role does faith play in the midst of these challenges?

WORKOUT

MATTHEW 6:25-30

Therefore I tell you, do not be anxious about your life, what you will eat or what you will drink, nor about your body, what you will put on. Is not life more than food, and the body more than clothing? Look at the birds of the air: they neither sow nor reap nor gather into barns, and yet your heavenly Father feeds them. Are you not of more value than they? And which of you by being anxious can add a single hour to his span of life? And why are you anxious about clothing? Consider the lilies of the field, how they grow: they neither toil nor spin, yet I tell you, even Solomon in all his glory was not arrayed like one of these. But if God so clothes the grass of the field, which today is alive and tomorrow is thrown into the oven, will he not much more clothe you, O you of little faith?

CONTEXT

Matthew 6 is in the middle of Jesus' famous Sermon on the Mount. He sat next to the Sea of Galilee and made one of the most profound statements ever spoken on dependence. Right after commanding people to lay up treasure in heaven, He comforts them with the reality that God the Father cares for His children.

EXPLORE THE MEANING

1. What stands out to you in this passage?
2. What does Jesus give as the antidote to anxiety?

MAN'S WAY OR GOD'S WAY?

Many coaches depend upon their own experience or advisors for wisdom at the exclusion of God. Man should depend on God because he is created, and a created being by nature is dependent on his creator. Peter reassures the believer that in all areas of life God has given us all we need through Christ and

His Word: "His divine power has granted to us all things that pertain to life and godliness" (2 Peter 1:3). Even when coaches think Christ needs to be part of their lives, they might believe He's an important part but not all. Some think they need Christ plus philosophy or they need Christ plus psychology. But the Bible says it's all in Christ and it's all in knowing Christ.

GOING DEEPER

1. Proverbs 3:5,6 says, "Trust in the Lord with all your heart, and do not lean on your own understanding. In all your ways acknowledge Him, and He will make straight your paths." How do these verses apply to coaching?
2. Second Peter 1:3 teaches that Jesus provides "all things that pertain to life and godliness." How does this apply to coaching?

COACHING GOD'S WAY

I can't imagine approaching each season without an attitude of dependence on God. For me, it all began when I turned away from the sin in my life and placed my trust and faith in Jesus Christ. This was shortly before my first coaching position at Brown University. Depending on God begins with understanding the Gospel or good news. What is the Gospel? The one and only God, who is holy, made us in His image to know Him. However, we have sinned and cut ourselves off from Him. Because of God's love for us, God became a man in Jesus, lived a perfect life, and died on the cross. He fulfilled the law himself by taking on the punishment we deserved for the sins of all those who ever turn and trust Him. He rose again from the dead, showing that God accepted Christ's sacrifice and that God's wrath against us had been exhausted. Now, God calls us to repent of our sins and trust in Christ; when we do we are born again into a new life, an eternal life with God.

ASSIGNMENT
- Bible reading: John chapter 6.
  Watch Lesson #4 @ www.kingdomsports.online

---- LESSON 5 ----

A LEADER SACRIFICES FOR OTHERS

"Greater love has no one than this, that someone lay down his life for his friends."

John 15:13

Wake Forest University baseball coach Tom Walter, "took one for the team" when he donated his kidney to freshman outfielder Kevin Jordan. "I feel I was meant to be here with Kevin," said 42-year-old Walter, whose players call him "Walt." "I don't consider myself a hero. It's just doing the right thing." During the winter of 2010, Jordan's health began to rapidly decline. Two days before he had enrolled at Wake Forest for the fall semester, doctors told Jordan he needed a kidney transplant as soon as possible. Jordan completed the first semester of school while receiving dialysis. While doctors discussed Jordan's treatment and prognosis with Walter and a trainer, "our mouths were hanging open," said Walter. "We couldn't believe what he had endured. I made the decision immediately that if I could help, I would." After Jordan's mother and brother were not found to be good donor matches, Walter was tested. Walter learned he was a match. When he told his team a week ago that he'd be donating his kidney, the players gave him an enthusiastic round of applause.

1. What are some of the sacrifices a coach makes?
2. What are the most important sacrifices a coach makes?

WARM UP

The Apostle Paul stated in Galatians 6:2 that we are to "bear the burdens of one another" as part of our requirements as a believer in Christ. We are not to live under a mindset of self-reliance, but by the commandment to really show we love one another sacrificially (John 13:34-35). The early church in Acts also modeled this sacrificial spirit. In Acts 2:42-47 we see the church actively engaged in caring and sharing of their resources. Clearly, the Lord is pleased when we show this type of active love.

True sacrificial love is demonstrated when we care for someone in a real and authentic way. Nothing...absolutely nothing, touches people like love. It breaks down internal competition. It makes others feel important. It silences gossip. It builds morale.

God will give you as a coach the opportunity to demonstrate sacrificial love to a variety of people ranging from players and coaches on your team to complete strangers. As He brings people across your path, you will have an opportunity to sacrifice for each of them.

1. What does it mean to "bear the burdens of one another?" Share examples.

2. Why is showing sacrificial love a big part of a Christian's life? How does sacrifice impact those who may not have a relationship with Christ?

3. Discuss the following statement: "You may be a highly knowledgeable coach and a dynamic motivator, but if you don't love God first and foremost, you will not be pleasing to Him. Your coaching will not be godly or spirit-empowered." —Gordon Thiessen

WORKOUT

ROMANS 5:6-11

For while we were still weak, at the right time Christ died for the ungodly. For one will scarcely die for a righteous person—though perhaps for a good person one would dare even to die—but God shows his love for us in that while we were still sinners, Christ died for us. Since, therefore, we have now been justified by his blood, much more shall we be saved by him from the wrath of God. For if while we were enemies we were reconciled to God by the death of his Son, much more, now that we are reconciled, shall we be saved by his life. More than that, we also rejoice in God through our Lord Jesus Christ, through whom we have now received reconciliation.

CONTEXT

The Apostle Paul is building on his argument that peace with God comes through faith in Jesus Christ. He traces peace with God all the way back to Abraham in Romans 4. It has always been about faith in the Messiah and always will be. Here in Romans 5, Paul explains that one of the most miraculous things about the sacrifice of Christ is that it was for His enemies.

EXPLORE THE MEANING

1. What stands out to you in this passage? How could you sum up the meaning of this passage in your own words?
2. What does it mean that "Christ died for the ungodly"?

MAN'S WAY OR GOD'S WAY?

What motivates you to sacrifice time and energy for your athletes? Maybe it's a desire to help your athletes, a sense of duty, and/or the enjoyment of teaching? There are many reasons a coach might sacrifice for his team. For the Christian coach, the primary reason must be love. It is the greatest and most consistent motivating power in sports. Everything God has done for the believer, including Christ's death for man's sin, is based on love. No one has ever given so much for a people so unworthy. It is not even that people were simply bad; they were full-blown enemies. Yet, Christ died for His people and conquered death so they may have life.

GOING DEEPER

1. Christian coaching is to be motivated by a threefold love: Christ's love for us, our love for Christ and love for others. Discuss how this applies to your coaching.
2. How does Jesus' death and resurrection impact your life?

COACHING GOD'S WAY

My desire to sacrifice for others begins when I fully understand the magnitude of God's sacrifice. The Apostle Paul taught this in Romans 12:1, "I appeal to you therefore, brothers, by the mercies of God, to present your bodies as a living sacrifice, holy and acceptable to God, which is your spiritual worship." The key to spiritual victory is not getting all you can get, but giving all you have. First of all, offering myself to God as a living sacrifice implies that my soul has been given to God. My willingness to sacrifice for others comes from that understanding. Next, what are the mercies of God? I believe the mercies of God are everything that God has done for the believer. The entire thing, all the provision of God's mercy for man's sin, all of it. By understanding God's mercy for me, I'm motivated to live a sacrificial life for others rather than trying to selfishly advance my own agenda.

ASSIGNMENT
- Bible reading: John chapters 7-8.
  Watch Lesson #5 @ www.kingdomsports.online

LESSON 6

A LEADER IS CONFIDENT

"But thanks be to God, who always leads us in triumph in Christ."

2 Corinthians 2:14

During the majority of his quarterback career with the Huskers, the late Brook Berringer spent his time as a backup to 1995 All-American Tommie Frazier, but he chose not to let it bother him. Brook's opportunity to start came during Nebraska's '94 championship run when Frazier was sidelined with a blood clot behind his right knee. Brook started, and his team won the final seven games. But in 1995 with Frazier healthy, he found himself again on the sideline. And though Berringer possessed the ability to start almost anywhere else in the country, he never publicly complained about it. He was a team player. "He handled a tough situation as well as and with about as much dignity as anybody ever could. As coaches, we have tried to help our players remain confident regardless of their circumstances. It's not possible to be an effective leader and be pessimistic." said Head Coach Tom Osborne. For Brook, his source of confidence and contentment was his faith in Jesus Christ. "When I have something more specific to focus on, like my faith and my desire to grow in that faith, it brings everything into focus," said Brook.

1. How do most players usually respond when being demoted?

2. What has been your experience coaching a confident athlete like Brook? How did that impact your team?

WARM UP

Confidence is placing full trust and belief in the reliability of a person or a thing. Confidence in the Lord is crucial to our Christian walk, but many athletes and coaches place their trust in their own abilities. Even many Christian coaches and athletes are tempted to revert to the habit of self-confidence.

Too often we are dependent on the external things of life, like our win and loss record, in governing our relationship with God. This is not the way God designed it. As believers we have the unchanging, steady, indwelling presence of Jesus Christ who is the same "yesterday, today and tomorrow."

Good coaches ooze confidence. Lord Montgomery wrote, "Leadership is the capacity and will to rally men and women to a common purpose, and the character which inspires confidence." Even if confidence isn't a part of your natural skill set, you can place confidence in God who is able to provide it.

Our confidence must be in the Savior, who has kept us from the grip of sin and death, and guaranteed our eternal life. And our confidence is to be in Him for the time in-between as well.

1. Identify a coach who is confident. What makes him/her a confident person?

2. Are you a confident person? Why or why not? What is the basis of your confidence?

3. Would you describe your team as confident? Why or why not?

4. In 1 Corinthians 2, Paul reminds the church that he did not come to them with persuasive words of wisdom, but in the strength of the Lord. He wanted them to have faith that "would not rest on the wisdom of men, but on the power of God" (v.5). How can this apply to coaching?

WORKOUT

ROMANS 8:28-30

And we know that for those who love God all things work together for good, for those who are called according to his purpose. For those whom he foreknew he also predestined to be conformed to the image of his Son, in order that he might be the firstborn among many brothers. And those whom he predestined he also called, and those whom he called he also justified, and those whom he justified he also glorified.

CONTEXT

The book of Romans is an incredible letter written by the Apostle Paul to the members of the church in Rome. More than any other person, Paul was responsible for the spread of Christianity throughout the Roman Empire. His main reason for writing the letter was to teach the great truths of the Gospel of grace. Paul explains and illustrates how sinners are credited the righteousness of Christ because of His substitutionary life, death and resurrection. Here in Romans 8, Paul is teaching that our future glory awaits believers and in light of this great hope, we should be encouraged and motivated to handle all the sufferings that life throws our way.

EXPLORE THE MEANING

1. What stands out to you in this passage? How could you sum up the meaning of this passage in your own words?
2. Why does Paul link our confidence to our future glory? How would this motivate someone going through trials?

MAN'S WAY OR GOD'S WAY?

Most athletes and coaches know that personal confidence is crucial to keep a team going. However, finding the right balance is not always easy. In fact, many individuals and teams are either over-confident or lack confidence. When confidence is based on our abilities or circumstances, there will always be a lack of consistency. From God's perspective, we can have confidence that He will accomplish His purposes in us because He loves us and has chosen to conform us to the image of His Son. It is in this reality that we can have confidence in any and every trial.

GOING DEEPER

1. Confidence is rooted in Gospel truth. How can you communicate this truth to others?
2. How does Romans 8:28-30 bring perspective to your team's wins and loses?

COACHING GOD'S WAY

We began this lesson with a story about Brook Berringer, who I (Ron Brown), recruited to Nebraska. I will never forget the transformation that took place in his life following his conversion to Christ. Like many players that I have counseled, he was pessimistic when he realized he had lost his starting position. I shared with him, as I do all my players, that the only reason for optimism or confidence is a relationship with Christ. This type of confidence is circumstance-free! It doesn't depend on a starting spot or a winning season. Brook went from being pessimistic to being confident after he placed his trust and faith in Christ. He became our most valuable player during his senior year while playing backup quarterback. While Brook might have been the least likely person on the team to be confident, he fixed his hope on the promise of triumph. His confidence was contagious. His leadership from the bench helped propel our team to the National Championship.

ASSIGNMENT

- Bible reading: John chapters 9-10.
  Watch Lesson #6 @ www.kingdomsports.online

---- LESSON 7 ----

A LEADER IS TRUTHFUL

"Rather, speaking the truth in love, we are to grow up in every way into him who is the head, into Christ,"

Ephesians 4:15

Political correctness has complicated our lives, not to mention made coaching more difficult. Many of us have trouble saying what we really mean and meaning what we really say! We are so afraid of hurting someone's feelings, we back away from confrontation which would clarify issues, solve problems, and heal relationships. Mike Krzyzewski is an outstanding basketball coach at Duke University. He spoke of truthfulness in his book *A Season Is a Lifetime:* "When your life span is only eight short months, you're always aware of the pressures of time. There is simply no time to waste. We can't always take the nice, polite way of saying things to each other; we need to communicate in ways that are more direct than most people are used to. We can only do this if we learn to trust each other and to understand that we're not trying to hurt each other with our words, even when to someone outside our team they might seem destructive. I tell our players we can always deal with the truth; don't lie or cheat yourself or others. Being straightforward gets everyone on the same page quickly. Honesty helps develop in our individual and team character a strong sense of integrity."

1. Why can it be difficult for coaches to be truthful?
2. What types of issues are made more complicated by telling the truth?

WARM UP

Truthfulness means earning future trust by accurately reporting past facts. Someone once said, "Tell the truth, and you can forget about it. Tell a lie, and you will have to remember it forever." Telling the truth brings freedom, but lies always entangle.

We sometimes whitewash our lies by calling them "unimportant" or by saying "everyone does it," but every lie leads directly and indirectly to more lies. In addition, there are the everyday exaggerations that eat away at a person's credibility. Words like always, never, best, most, and biggest often aren't true. Exaggerations erode a person's future trustworthiness.

The primary consequence of deception is the loss of trust. Living falsely betrays our friends, family, coaching staff, players and anyone else who discovers our lie. When individuals are not trustworthy, they will find themselves becoming more and more isolated. Trust is a vital part of any lasting and meaningful relationship. Conversely, damaging trust is one of the most difficult things to restore.

Make it your goal to clear your record with others. Commit yourself to speaking the truth, even if it means going against popular opinion. Remember, the trail of truthfulness leads to true success, and it does set you free.

1. Where do you go to look for truth?

2. Why is truthfulness a vital quality for a successful coach?

3. How truthful are those you compete with and against in your sport? Is it more difficult to be truthful with yourself, others or God? Why?

WORKOUT

EPHESIANS 4:17-25

Now this I say and testify in the Lord, that you must no longer walk as the Gentiles do, in the futility of their minds. They are darkened in their understanding, alienated from the life of God because of the ignorance that is in them, due to their hardness of heart. They have become callous and have given themselves up to sensuality, greedy to practice every kind of impurity. But that is not the way you learned Christ! –assuming that you have heard about him and were taught in him, as the truth is in Jesus, to put off your old self, which belongs to your former manner of life and is corrupt through deceitful desires, and to be renewed in the spirit of your minds, and to put on the new self, created after the likeness of God in true righteousness and holiness. Therefore, having put away falsehood, let each one of you speak the truth with his neighbor, for we are members one of another.

CONTEXT

The Bible continually uses the phrase "walk" as a way of describing one's life. In Ephesians 4, Paul calls Christians to walk in a manner worthy of their calling. They are to put off their old life and put on the new self. One of the first characteristics of this new life is truthfulness.

EXPLORE THE MEANING

1. What stood out to you in this passage?

2. What does it mean for a coach to put off the old self?

3. Discuss how Christians are different from the world in this passage.

MAN'S WAY OR GOD'S WAY?

In recent years, there have been too many examples of coaches who have not been truthful when dealing with their athletes and fans. Many coaches will avoid being truthful to protect themselves and their programs. However, the Apostle Paul commands all believers to put away falsehood...but he doesn't stop there, he adds: "let each one of you speak truth with his neighbor." This is helpful language, showing that we must not only cast off sinful habits but put on godly ones.

GOING DEEPER

1. What does truthfulness to your athletes look like?
2. How has the truth of the Gospel changed your life? How different do you look now?

COACHING GOD'S WAY

Many coaches want their athletes to like them. However, if the desire to be popular is too strong, it can lead to flattery and compromise. In other words, a coach needs to be truthful and not flatter his athletes. Usually, an athlete will become suspicious of a coach who doesn't talk straight with him. Jesus' answer to the rich man's question in Mark 10:17-22 was straightforward. He wanted him to understand that he couldn't possibly gain eternal life by his doing since he would need to keep all of the commandments, and keep them in the fullest sense. He wanted him to see that no living man can possibly do this to be saved. He was showing him the error in his thinking so he could be saved. As coaches, we need to be truthful with our athletes and help them learn from their mistakes.

ASSIGNMENT
- Bible reading: John chapters 11-12.
  Watch Lesson #7 @ www.kingdomsports.online

---- LESSON 8 ----

A LEADER IS POISED

"And Jesus grew in wisdom and stature, and in favor with God and men."

Luke 2:52

Poise means "balance" or "stability," also "ease and dignity of manner." Here are two stories of coaches who believed poise was one of the most important traits of a successful athlete.

John Wooden often preached poise to his players. He said, "Self-control in little things leads to control of bigger things. For example, the reason I prohibited profanity during practices was because it was usually caused by frustration or anger. I felt that a player who couldn't control his language when he got upset during a scrimmage would be more likely to lose control in more damaging ways during the heat of a competition." During the 2006 volleyball season, John Cook's Nebraska volleyball team overcame a two game deficit in the regional finals. The media and fans wondered what Coach Cook told his players in the locker room during the break. He said, "Our team showed great poise coming back to win the Final Four. With so much on the line, we won the final three games and the match. That team was a great example of poise as they were able to handle the pressure because many of our players relied on the Lord so they were less anxious about their performances."

1. How does a coach's poise impact his athletes?
2. When have you seen poise determine the outcome of a game?

WARM UP

Talk about "poise" comes up often in big-time sporting events. After a key win, coaches will comment on how their team maintained poise in the midst of a demanding situation. Poise is a key character quality because it reveals whether or not you are balanced.

The dictionary defines poise as "a state of balance or equilibrium; dignified and composed in all situations."

Rarely do we find a person who is well-balanced and poised. Charles Jefferson said, "The average man is one-sided, unsymmetrical and unevenly developed." It is rare to find a person who has a balanced mind and spirit.

In every person there is either something lacking or too much of something, which creates a character flaw. But Jesus was without flaw—He never lacked nor did He go to extremes. He had unrivaled poise in conduct. Charles Hummel is his book, "Tyranny of the Urgent" tells us how Jesus Christ maintained His poise. The key to His success was that He received His daily instructions in quiet moments with the Father. Nothing came in the way of His intimate time with God. If Jesus needed this time with God, how much more do you and I need to seek it out? Yes, my ability to live life filled with poise is directly related to my time alone with God.

1. Why is being poised (or balanced) extremely important to the success of a team? Do you believe you and your team are poised? Why?

2. What can you learn from Christ's poise related to your own coaching career?

3. Describe your own personal quiet time with the Lord. Do you get daily instructions from God? What happens when you do and don't?

WORKOUT

LUKE 20:1-8

One day, as Jesus was teaching the people in the temple and preaching the gospel, the chief priests and the scribes with the elders came up and said to him, "Tell us by what authority you do these things, or who it is that gave you this authority." He answered them, "I also will ask you a question. Now tell me, was the baptism of John from heaven or from man?" And they discussed it with one another, saying, "If we say, 'From heaven,' he will say, 'Why did you not believe him?' But if we say, 'From man,' all the people will stone us to death, for they are convinced that John was a prophet." So they answered that they did not know where it came from. And Jesus said to them, "Neither will I tell you by what authority I do these things."

CONTEXT

Luke 20 includes a series of carefully coordinated attacks on Christ by the Jewish leaders who designed their questions to entrap Him. These leaders included the chief priests, scribes, and elders—key representatives of the elite Sanhedrin. These men were from a large council in Jerusalem, consisting of seventy-one prominent religious leaders, collectively known as the Sanhedrin. They had ultimate authority over Israel in all religious and spiritual matters and even Caesar recognized this authority in some civil affairs. Luke contrasts their authority with Jesus Christ, who has supreme authority over all things.

EXPLORE THE MEANING

1. What stood out to you in this passage?
2. Have you ever been questioned about authority that was rightfully yours? When? Why? How did you react?
3. How were the Pharisees trying to trap Jesus with their question in Luke 20:2? How did Jesus demonstrate poise?

MAN'S WAY OR GOD'S WAY?

True poise is possible for anyone who relies on God's strength and spirit. J.I. Packer wrote, "If your eyes are filled with light and working properly, your body will be able to move easily and safely. If you can't see clearly, you will lack physical ease and poise. Similarly, if your heart is possessed by what this world and this life offers, you will not be able to see spiritual issues clearly, and when you read the Bible, its full meaning will escape you."

GOING DEEPER

1. Why did Jesus answer the religious leaders with another question? How did his question stump them? How did they finally respond to Jesus? What was religious leaders real motive? How did Jesus' poise help Him respond to their question?
2. What can you apply from this lesson to your coaching?

COACHING GOD'S WAY

Poise is the idea of letting the peace of Christ rule in your heart. When I'm surrounded by 80,000 screaming football fans, it's important for me to remain absolutely calm no matter what happens. When my players begin to lose confidence and become anxious, that's when they need me to remain unperturbed. Consider Jesus in the Gospels. He moves into every situation with total poise. He is not upset by others but remains calm and collected when other people are panicking around him. He is in control. The peace of God is produced by the Spirit of God along with the Word of God.

ASSIGNMENT
- Bible reading: John chapters 13,14.
  Watch Lesson #8 @ www.kingdomsports.online

---— LESSON 9 ———

A LEADER IS PURPOSEFUL

"So whatever you eat or drink, or whatever you do, do all to the glory of God."

1 Corinthians 10:31

UTEP Coach Don Haskins had a specific purpose with his starting line-up in the 1966 NCAA National Championship basketball game in College Park, Maryland. Facing the top-ranked University of Kentucky in the championship game, Haskins made history by starting five African-American players for the first time in a championship game against Kentucky's all-white squad, coached by Adolph Rupp. The UTEP Miners beat Kentucky 72-65, winning the tournament and finishing the year with a 28-1 record. While wanting to place his best players on the court, he also knew there was another purpose which would motivate his players to win the game. His opponent had won five national championships and still refused to recruit black players. Hours before the game, Haskins told his team that he heard Coach Rupp vow that "no five blacks are going to beat Kentucky." Were the Miners motivated?

"Kentucky was playing for a commemorative wristwatch and the right to say they were national champions," said Harry Flournoy, who averaged 8.3 points and 10.7 rebounds for UTEP. "We were out to prove that it didn't matter what color a person's skin was."

1. What are reasons that motivate coaches and athletes?
2. What are the problems with some of these reasons?

WARM UP

There is always a reason, a motivation, for whatever we do. In fact, the word "motivation" means "to provide with a reason," or "to incite to action." We may never have expressed our purpose (motivation), but whether it is selfish (to win games, to obtain more money, or a better job) or unselfish (to help athletes achieve their potential), we always have a purpose.

In athletic contests, a coach prepares a game plan ahead of time. God designed a plan for your life before the world began. God is holy and perfect. He created us to love Him, glorify Him, and enjoy Him forever. God's plan involved His Son, Jesus Christ. Jesus willingly sacrificed His life so each of us could have a right relationship with God. He went to the cross and shed His blood to pay the penalty for our sin. This act of love fulfilled the plan and purpose of God.

God's plans will not be thwarted. His purpose includes you having a relationship with Jesus Christ (read John 3:16 and 1 John 3:16). God's goal is for you to understand your sin, repent of it, and turn to Christ in faith. Ultimately, life outside of knowing, loving and serving Christ will result in a meaningless existence without purpose.

1. Would you describe yourself as a "purposeful" person? Why or why not?

2. Why does God deserve glory based on Psalm 100:3, "It is He who has made us."?

3. Since God's glory can't be added to or increased in any way, why do we speak of bringing glory to God?

WORKOUT

JOHN 12:36-43

So Jesus said to them, "The light is among you for a little while longer. Walk while you have the light, lest darkness overtake you. The one who walks in the darkness does not know where he is going. While you have the light, believe in the light, that you may become sons of light. "When Jesus had said these things, he departed and hid himself from them. Though he had done so many signs before them, they still did not believe in him, so that the word spoken by the prophet Isaiah might be fulfilled: "Lord, who has believed what he heard from us, and to whom has the arm of the Lord been revealed?" Therefore they could not believe. For again Isaiah said, He has blinded their eyes and hardened their heart, lest they see with their eyes, and understand with their heart, and turn, and I would heal them." Isaiah said these things because he saw his glory and spoke of him. Nevertheless, many even of the authorities believed in him, but for fear of the Pharisees they did not confess it, so that they would not be put out of the synagogue; for they loved the glory that comes from man more than the glory that comes from God.

CONTEXT

John lists two causes for Israel's unbelief, one divine and the other human. They illustrate the interface between divine sovereignty and human responsibility. The personal or human choice involved in rejecting Jesus Christ is illustrated by the rulers who believed in Him. They were not confessing Him because they feared rejection from the Pharisees; therefore their faith was inadequate. They wanted the approval or glory of man more than the glory that comes from God.

EXPLORE THE MEANING

1. What stood out to you in the passage?

2. Is there anyone or group that coaches often fear? Why?

MAN'S WAY OR GOD'S WAY?

Many coaches find purpose in their career through bringing glory to themselves, their schools, or the community. Others like Don Haskins find purpose by helping to integrate college basketball or win a national championship. While these might be noble reasons to coach, nothing compares to coaching for the glory of God. Jesus is the definition of a person having purpose. Luke records that He set his face toward Jerusalem (9:51) even though it meant that He would die. Jesus' sole purpose was to please His Heavenly Father.

GOING DEEPER

1. What are examples of coaches seeking their own glory?
2. How can a coach reflect and amplify God's glory to others?

COACHING GOD'S WAY

During my coaching career, I have learned that glorifying God involves bearing "much fruit" as described in John 15:8. It helps me to break it down into two categories. First, it begins with the correct attitude. I like to call this "Attitude Fruit" based on the fruit of the Spirit in Galatians 5:22-23. This allows others to see the results of a Spirit-filled life. Second, it is connected to "Action Fruit" or right action (Philippians 1:9-11). It's both the right attitude and the right action that leads to reflecting the glory of God through coaching. It's being more concerned with God's approval than man's approval. God's glory must be our primary goal in everything and it begins with a willingness to sacrifice self and self-glory.

ASSIGNMENT
- Bible reading: John chapters 15-16.
  Watch Lesson #9 @ www.kingdomsports.online

---- LESSON 10 ----

A LEADER IS SELF-CONTROLLED

"A man without self-control is like a city broken into and left without walls."

Proverbs 25:28

Jim Harbaugh charged across the field, lifting his shirt to expose his belly to attempt a chest bump. He extended his right hand to Jim Schwartz for a shake and slapped him on the back with his left hand. Schwartz didn't like what was done or said—claiming he heard an expletive—and went charging after Harbaugh. What an emotional scene following a hyped-up, high-profile meeting of turnaround teams in San Francisco's 25-19 victory over Detroit! After the incident, both coaches offered apologies for their actions. "That is totally on me," Harbaugh said. "I shook his hand too hard. I really went in, and it was a strong, kind of a slap-grab handshake."

"It's unfortunate," Schwartz told reporters. "The game is played by the players on the field. We certainly don't want things like that to occur. There are competitive people in the league, and I think we need to do a better job of just leaving it to the players on the field."

1. Describe a game or practice when you lost self-control. What resulted from your loss of control?
2. Describe a time when you displayed tremendous self-control. What happened in this situation?

WARM UP

Developing self-control isn't easy. Pastor John Piper said, "Following Christ isn't magic. It requires repeated actions on our part, which develop into habits and life disciplines." While the key to self-control isn't easy, it is possible for the Christ-centered believer who develops habits such as Bible reading, memorization and prayer.

Coaches and athletes who have great ability to concentrate, to focus, and to define and stay consistently within their priorities tend to be very successful in sports. Self-discipline is an essential component of their success. The bridge between a wish and reality is self-control, a fruit of the Spirit. The Apostle Paul taught this in Galatians 5:22-23, "But the fruit of the Spirit is love, joy, peace, patience, kindness, goodness, faithfulness, gentleness, self-control; against such things there is no law."

It is possible for discipline to produce self-control only as we yield to God's Spirit. This results in new habits and behavior. Spirit-control and self-control are connected in the Bible. Godly self-control is only possible by submitting to God's Spirit. One of my friends defined self-control as "love under control." Because of the love we have experienced first-hand through Jesus Christ, we can exhibit self-control rather than becoming angry or bitter.

1. Name a coach who has great self-control. How does self-control help him/her?

2. What is an area relating to a person, place or thing that really frustrates you?

3. Our temper can get us into lots of hot water. Share a time when this happened in your life. What was the ultimate result of having a lack of self-control?

WORKOUT

1 CORINTHIANS 10:6-13

Now these things took place as examples for us, that we might not desire evil as they did. Do not be idolaters as some of them were; as it is written, "The people sat down to eat and drink and rose up to play." We must not indulge in sexual immorality as some of them did, and twenty-three thousand fell in a single day. We must not put Christ to the test, as some of them did and were destroyed by serpents, nor grumble, as some of them did and were destroyed by the Destroyer. Now these things happened to them as an example, but they were written down for our instruction, on whom the end of the ages has come. Therefore let anyone who thinks that he stands take heed lest he fall. No temptation has overtaken you that is not common to man. God is faithful, and he will not let you be tempted beyond your ability, but with the temptation he will also provide the way of escape, that you may be able to endure it.

CONTEXT

One of the main ways to fall into temptation and sin is to become overconfident. Many of the Corinthian believers felt perfectly secure in their Christian lives, with a mindset that they had arrived. In this passage, Paul reminds them to be careful not to become overconfident. Paul used Israel as an example of the dangers of overconfidence. Earlier in 1 Corinthians 10, he uses their forty-year wandering between Egypt and Canaan as an example of the pitfalls of overconfidence.

EXPLORE THE MEANING

1. What stood out to you in this passage?
2. In what areas can believers become overconfident?
3. What would be an example of a coach who becomes overconfident in his spiritual walk? What is the result?

MAN'S WAY OR GOD'S WAY?

Even unbelieving coaches view self-control as a necessary part of sports to be successful. In Jesus' day, the word translated "self-control" was used to describe athletes. Those who were successful abstained from certain activities for the sake of disciplined training exercises. For the Christian coach, self-control is about pleasing God so that it's possible to control his desires rather than allowing them to control him.

GOING DEEPER

1. What are some practices that have helped you develop self-control? Discuss some of these practices: 1. Be on time. 2. Organize your life. 3. Do the hardest thing first.
2. How can pursuing discipline in some of these areas carry over to the spiritual areas?

COACHING GOD'S WAY

Two emotions often associated with poor performance are anxiety and anger. I often remind my athletes that without self-control they will be defeated by these two emotions. This is the sort of self-control or self-denial the Apostle Paul taught in 1 Corinthians 9:27, "I discipline my body and bring it into subjection." He used a Greek expression that means "to strike under the eye." He was figuratively saying that he made his own body a punching bag in order to cultivate discipline. Paul never lost sight of his goal, and neither should we as Christian coaches. We need to keep the goal of being conformed to the image of Christ in view as we develop self-control in our lives.

ASSIGNMENT
- Bible reading: John chapters 17-18.
  Watch Lesson #10 @ www.kingdomsports.online

---- LESSON 11 ----

A LEADER IS ENERGETIC

"I can do all this through him who gives me strength."

Philippians 4:13

At the age of 38, Dick Vermeil had the college football world in the palm of his hand. The young coach from the West went east and became the head coach of the Philadelphia Eagles in 1976. Five years later, his Eagles were in their first Super Bowl. He was named the NFL's Coach of the Year in 1980, and led the Eagles into Super Bowl XV after defeating the Dallas Cowboys for the NFC championship. He retired for the first time after the 1982 season citing "severe burnout."

Fatigue has afflicted many coaches, including Urban Meyer. He made the surprising decision in 2010 to step down as head football coach at Florida after a very successful career, citing the overall grind of coaching and the toll it took on his personal life. The life of a coach is a unique career experience when compared to more traditional jobs—especially with high profile coaching positions. Coaches like Meyer enjoy the benefits that come with coaching, but also struggle to find time in their lives to spend with families because of being "on the job" 24/7 during their seasons.

1. What wears you down during your season?
2. What advice regarding priorities would you give to a coach just beginning his/her career?

WARM UP

Have you ever known a successful coach who lacked energy? The words "lazy" and "idle" are not part of a coach's vocabulary. Coaches must be industrious and diligent to lead their teams. The good coach, like the good athlete, has to reach deep within and find a way to persevere when they are weary and facing all kinds of trials.

The Apostle Paul faced both weariness and every possible type of trial during his mission trips, but he relied on the Lord for his energy. Paul said, "I can do all things through Christ who strengthens me" (Philippians 4:13). That's why he was able to write in verse 12, "I know how to be brought low, and I know how to abound. In any and every circumstance, I have learned the secret of facing plenty and hunger, abundance and need."

Paul would not be controlled by his body. That's the key to running the Christian race with endurance. Throughout Paul's writings, he referred to the sin principle as "the flesh." It's the idea that the "body" is itself not inherently evil, but it's the evil desires that are associated with the body. Paul said we should, "put to death the deeds of the body (Romans 8:13).

1. When Urban Meyer returned to coach at Ohio State, he first signed another contract with his family It included regular exercise, eat three meals at day, see his family and limit the hours spent coaching. What other priorities would you add to these? Why?

2. The spiritual life of a Christian is much more like a marathon run than a sprint. What kind of strength do you need to run a marathon race? What kind of strength does your coaching staff and team need from you?

3. Read Philippians 4:13. Can we really do everything through Christ who gives us strength? How can you and your team learn to rely on the strength of Christ?

WORKOUT

PHILIPPIANS 4:10-19

I rejoiced in the Lord greatly that now at length you have revived your concern for me. You were indeed concerned for me, but you had no opportunity. Not that I am speaking of being in need, for I have learned in whatever situation I am to be content. I know how to be brought low, and I know how to abound. In any and every circumstance, I have learned the secret of facing plenty and hunger, abundance and need. I can do all things through him who strengthens me. Yet it was kind of you to share my trouble. And you Philippians yourselves know that in the beginning of the gospel, when I left Macedonia, no church entered into partnership with me in giving and receiving, except you only. Even in Thessalonica you sent me help for my needs once and again. Not that I seek the gift, but I seek the fruit that increases to your credit. I have received full payment, and more. I am well supplied, having received from Epaphroditus the gifts you sent, a fragrant offering, a sacrifice acceptable and pleasing to God. And my God will supply every need of yours according to his riches in glory in Christ Jesus.

CONTEXT

The Apostle Paul teaches his readers the secret of contentment here in Philippians. Contentment relates directly to how much energy or weariness we feel in adversity. The Bible has a lot to say about being content. Paul said in 1 Timothy 6:6, "Godliness with contentment is great gain." Most people seek contentment and assume that contentment is the absence of all problems. That's not the true meaning of contentment. If it were, no one would ever have it because you can't be completely free from problems. True contentment is being able to be satisfied and content in the midst of any problem. That's the kind of contentment God offers through Christ.

EXPLORE THE MEANING

1. What stood out to you in the passage?

2. How does contentment relate to spiritual burnout?

MAN'S WAY OR GOD'S WAY?

Some coaches look forward to their off-season to refresh themselves and recover from the pressures of coaching. While it's important to get the necessary rest, the Christian coach knows his true rest and satisfaction is related to living life through understanding the providence of God. Resting in God's promise brings satisfaction as we look forward to our eternal home in Heaven.

GOING DEEPER

1. What is the connection between Christ providing the strength to live the Christian life and contentment?
2. How can a coach be content without becoming complacent?

COACHING GOD'S WAY

Our sufficiency comes from being attached to the sufficient one. As Christian coaches, we are not to be self-sufficient, we are to be Christ-sufficient. Since we're linked to His life and linked to His power in us we have sufficiency. Paul is saying, "Look, I can do all things through Him who strengthens me." What does he mean? It doesn't mean that my athletes become supermen! It means we're connected to Christ so He lives in us. God promises to provide supernatural strength in every circumstance.

ASSIGNMENT
- Bible reading: John chapter 19.
  Watch Lesson #11 @ www.kingdomsports.online

---- LESSON 12 ----

A LEADER IS DETERMINED

*"I have fought the good fight,
I have finished the race, I have kept the faith."*

2 Timothy 4:7

Prior to the 2011-12 season, 59-year old basketball coach Pat Summitt had won eight NCAA National Championships and 1,071 games. With her famous icy glare, she recently announced she would continue coaching as she stares down early-onset Alzheimer's Disease. As Summitt entered her 39th season as coach at the University of Tennessee, she was diagnosed in May 2011 and told the world. Reaction was shock giving way to dismay, tempered by admiration for her fighting spirit.

Summitt wrote an open letter to the university community. "I plan to continue to be your coach," she wrote. "Obviously, I realize I may have some limitations with this condition since there will be some good days and some bad days. For that reason, I will be relying on my outstanding coaching staff like never before." That is perhaps the only known quantity in all this. What lies ahead is mostly about the unknown—how her condition might progress, how stress might affect it, and how her players might react to all the attention focused on the health of their coach.

1. Do you think coaches are more determined than others? Why or why not?

WARM UP

Determination is working intently to accomplish goals regardless of the opposition. Determination is the resolve to keep going in spite of roadblocks. No matter how daunting the task, determined people finish the job.

In Philippians 3:12,14, Paul tells us to press on for the goal and the prize found in Christ Jesus. God calls us to never go backward. Attempt something great for God, and do it with all your might. Few things are more rewarding than the exhilaration of achievement after wholehearted effort. The stronger the current opposing us, the sweeter the victory.

Christians need to persist against a variety of obstacles. We are never finished until the race is done. Our adversary, the devil, tries to discourage us constantly, but through determination we can accomplish our goals in spite of a variety of obstacles.

1. How much do you listen to "naysayers" and those who talk negatively? How can you best respond with an attitude of determination?

2. Have you ever felt like quitting something but then did not? How did it make you feel to pursue, to keep going? How does quitting impact other people?

3. How do you respond when your determined efforts are shattered? Where do you go to find hope?

4. Describe a time when you or your team showed great determination. What ultimately happened?

5. What are the keys to determination?

6. How do you teach determination to your athletes?

WORKOUT

PHILIPPIANS 3:12-16

Not that I have already obtained this or am already perfect, but I press on to make it my own, because Christ Jesus has made me his own. Brothers, I do not consider that I have made it my own. But one thing I do: forgetting what lies behind and straining forward to what lies ahead, I press on toward the goal for the prize of the upward call of God in Christ Jesus. Let those of us who are mature think this way, and if in anything you think otherwise, God will reveal that also to you. Only let us hold true to what we have attained.

CONTEXT

The Apostle Paul uses the analogy of a runner to describe the Christian's spiritual growth. Since believers have not reached their goal of Christlikeness, they must continue to pursue it like the runner in a race. This goal of becoming like Christ is repeated many times in the Bible and is clear from passages like Romans 8:29, "For those He foreknew He also predestined to be conformed to the image of His Son, in order that He might be the firstborn among many brothers."

EXPLORE THE MEANING

1. What is the upward call of God?

2. How is Paul determined to meet this goal?

3. How is it possible to forget what lies behind?

MAN'S WAY OR GOD'S WAY?

Many coaches pursue goals that will only disappoint and frustrate them throughout their careers, but the Christian coach should have a much greater goal. Just as the Apostle Paul was still striving with the purpose of being Christlike, how much more should we be striving to be like our Savior? Christlikeness should be our goal in all we do. We should be determined to obtain it and press forward at all times. Paul was determined to be obedient so as to not disqualify himself from the prize. He had a goal and was determined to meet it.

GOING DEEPER

1. What are the common goals many coaches spend their lives pursuing? How can these be disappointing?

2. Are most coaches determined to become more like Christ? Why or why not?

3. How difficult is it to "press on" in life?

COACHING GOD'S WAY

The Greek word for "press on" in Philippians 3:12 was used of a sprinter, and refers to aggressive, energetic action. The Apostle Paul was pursuing his goal of becoming like Christ with all his strength, straining every spiritual muscle to win the prize. As a coach and former athlete, I can relate to Paul's aggressive pursuit of his goal. Each season, our coaching staff lays out individual and team goals for the year. However, for the Christian athlete or coach, nothing should take the place of our ultimate goal, which is becoming like Christ. I'm determined to help our team reach its goals, but nothing compares with our ultimate purpose as believers to conform to God's glorious image. This was not only Paul's goal, but should be the goal every Christian coach should strive to attain.

ASSIGNMENT
- Bible reading: John chapters 20, 21.
  Watch Lesson #12 @ www.kingdomsports.online

SECTION TWO

BUILDING LEADERSHIP CHARACTER
COACH'S EDITION
30 MINUTES

LESSON 1

A LEADER IS LOYAL

*"Many a man proclaims his own loyalty,
but who can find a trustworthy man?"*

Proverbs 20:6

When Tom Osborne retired, more than 700 players and coaches who had been part of the Nebraska football program attended his retirement banquet. Their devotion and loyalty toward the man they simply called "Coach" was clearly in response to the admiration and loyalty instilled in them. During his career, the average tenure for Osborne's assistant coaches was 14 years compared to three years at other schools. He was well known for standing behind his players and remaining loyal to them even when they got into trouble. Most famously, he continued to support Lawrence Phillips when most coaches would have given up on him. Phillips was the troubled running back who later had a brief career in the NFL. Speaking of Phillips, he said, "My faith has led me to believe that no person is exempt from the pull of God or beyond redemption, including Lawrence. One of the last times I saw Lawrence I gave him a New Testament and explained that the only solution I saw would involve a spiritual commitment."

1. What stands out to you in Coach Osborne's statement?

2. What was the motivation for Coach Osborne's handling of Lawrence Phillips? What is it about his faith that would compel Osborne to remain loyal to Phillips?

WORKOUT

JOHN 21:15-19

CONTEXT

This exchange between Peter and Jesus occurred after the crucifixion and resurrection and is known as the restoration of Peter. Prior to the death of Christ, Peter had proclaimed his loyalty to Jesus no matter the cost—even if all the others fell away, Peter swore that he would remain! And yet just a short time later Peter denied that he even knew who Jesus was, not once but three times! The Lord addressed Peter by his original name (Simon), as if he had forfeited the strength of his new name Peter, the rock, through denying Christ.

EXPLORE THE MEANING

1. What stands out to you in this passage?
2. Explain how Peter must have felt when he was questioned for the third time? Can you relate to this as a coach?

MAN'S WAY OR GOD'S WAY?

When adversity strikes, man-centered loyalty fails just as Peter's pledge did, but biblical loyalty is compelled by love and includes a commitment to God. It's built on the foundation of Jesus' demonstration of His loyal love for us, which in turn produces a love response of loyalty back to Him and those around us.

GOING DEEPER

1. Could you explain to someone where your greatest loyalty lies and why? How does your response compare to the Gospel message Christ presents?
2. As you think about Osborne's reason for supporting his player, how did the Gospel influence what he did?

LESSON 2

A LEADER IS A SERVANT-LEADER

"For even the Son of Man came not to be served but to serve, and to give his life as a ransom for many."

Mark 10:45

Over the years, the late Kay Yow (formerly of North Carolina State) and current Nevada Head Coach Jane Albright developed a close friendship. In *Leader of the Pack: The Legacy of Legendary Coach Kay Yow*, Albright recalls when Yow joined her family for one of many Christmas dinners. "On Christmas 2006, when Kay was right in the middle of her fight with cancer, we were all scared she would not be able to come, but late that day she arrived, once again bearing special stories and gifts. Kay rarely talked about herself, but this Christmas she spoke of her battle with cancer and the hundreds of letters she had received from people who had prayed for her and wanted to encourage her. She explained that she didn't have the energy to respond to each letter. I quickly told her that all of these people, most of whom didn't know her personally, did not expect an answer to their words. 'But I at least want to answer the young people's letters,' she said. 'You know, letter writing is a dying thing now and I want to encourage them to write more of them.' Only Kay Yow would take something meant just for her and turn it back to the giver."

1. Describe a servant-coach in your own words.
2. What impact do athletes who model servant-leadership have on your team?

WORKOUT

MATTHEW 20:20-28

CONTEXT

This passage teaches both the right and wrong reasons for desiring leadership. James and John recruited their mother to present their proud and self-seeking request to Jesus. Since their mother was the sister of Jesus' mother, they very likely thought her appeal would influence Jesus' response. Even today, it's not uncommon for people to seek positions of leadership for reasons other than being the best qualified person for the job.

EXPLORE THE MEANING

1. What stands out to you in this passage?
2. What does a leader learn from about leadership from suffering?

MAN'S WAY OR GOD'S WAY?

In this passage of Scripture, the Lord teaches the disciples that the style of leadership for believers should be different than that of non-believers. The non-believing Gentile leaders dominated in a dictatorial style, using whatever means necessary to control their followers. This style of leadership is still common today among many coaches. However, true spiritual leadership means loving service to one another. The real leader is a coach who serves, not a coach who demands to be served.

GOING DEEPER

1. Jesus said, "...to give His life a ransom for many (v. 28). The word translated "for" means "in the place of." This verse shows the substitutionary nature of Christ's sacrifice. Further, a "ransom" is a price paid to redeem a slave. How does this apply to coaching?

---- LESSON 3 ----

A LEADER GUARDS THEIR HEART

"Keep your heart with all vigilance, for from it flow the springs of life"
Proverbs 4:23

Ohio State football's memorabilia-for-cash and tattoos scandal forced coach Jim Tressel to resign following a stellar career that included an overall record of 94–22. He failed to report information about players involved with the incident. Jason Wright a former NFL veteran, had this to say about Coach Tressel. "I believe Jim Tressel loves God. I believe he has faith that Jesus is the Son of God and the Savior of the world. I also believe that he has a real personal relationship with the one true God. During my time playing for the Cleveland Browns, I was repeatedly told of the stellar job he did representing the faith at churches, parachurch fundraisers, and other Christian gatherings. I've heard equally positive reports from his former players. And I don't think he was faking." While some fans might debate Wright's assessment, this is a reminder to all coaches that if something like this can happen to Jim Tressel, it can happen to any coach who fails to guard his heart.

1. While we can't know for sure Coach Tressel's motivation in failing to report the player violations, we do know it cost him his job. What are some temptations coaches face?
2. What makes it so difficult for coaches or athletes to admit their faults?

WORKOUT

MATTHEW 6:19-24

CONTEXT

It has been said that the Bible views the heart as the human mission control center. It is out of the heart that man operates. To the authors of the Bible, the heart was much more than an organ pumping blood or the emotionally driven concept that we have today. It involved all of oneself. Here Jesus is drilling down to what really matters by asking the most important question, "Who do you serve?" And this question has eternal consequences.

EXPLORE THE MEANING

1. What stands out to you in this passage?
2. Why does Jesus link one's desires to their pocketbook?
3. What matters most to coaches?

MAN'S WAY OR GOD'S WAY?

The relationship in this passage is that of a slave to a master. A slave cannot be owned by two people. However, many coaches spend their entire careers serving several masters. Even for the Christian coach this is a challenge. Scripture doesn't teach that a believer won't be tempted by idolatry and sin. How each person spends his time, talents and treasures, etc. will show who he is truly owned by. If you truly belong to Jesus, then you will guard your heart so that it seeks His glory above all things. So the question remains, are you storing up treasure in heaven or collecting wood, hay and stubble?

GOING DEEPER

1. What treasures might coaches store up for themselves?
2. What motivates you? How do you spend your time?

--- LESSON 4 ---

A LEADER DEPENDS ON GOD

"It does not, therefore, depend on man's desire or effort, but on God's mercy."

Romans 9:16

"Football is a profession that is judged by performance and results," says Tony Dungy, former head coach of the Indianapolis Colts. "However, those things come and go so quickly that as a coach, I had to depend on something more." Tony Dungy is a devout Christian who depends on God to strive for excellence. In his own words, what follows is his explanation of the source of his strength and character.

"When I went to the Steelers in 1977, there was a group of guys who were different than any I had ever been around—guys like Donnie Shell, Mel Blount, Jon Kolb and Larry Brown. They were very focused players who loved football and Jesus. As I watched them, I sensed something very unique, and I realized it was their relationship with Jesus Christ that made them different. Their decisions were based on Christ, because they believed He has the answers for everything. They helped me straighten out my priorities."

1. How are coaches and their families affected by other's judgment of performance and results?
2. Name a few coaches who have left coaching because the profession is so stressful and demanding,

WORKOUT

MATTHEW 6:25-30

CONTEXT

Matthew 6 is in the middle of Jesus' famous Sermon on the Mount. He sat next to the Sea of Galilee and made one of the most profound statements ever spoken on dependence. Right after commanding people to lay up treasure in heaven, He comforts them with the reality that God the Father cares for His children.

EXPLORE THE MEANING

1. What stands out to you in this passage?
2. What does Jesus give as the antidote to anxiety?

MAN'S WAY OR GOD'S WAY?

Many coaches depend upon their own experience or advisors for wisdom at the exclusion of God. Man should depend on God because he is created, and a created being by nature is dependent on his creator. Peter reassures the believer that in all areas of life God has given us all we need through Christ and His Word: "His divine power has granted to us all things that pertain to life and godliness" (2 Peter 1:3). Even when coaches think Christ needs to be part of their lives, they might believe He's an important part but not all. Some think they need Christ plus philosophy or they need Christ plus psychology. But the Bible says it's all in Christ and it's all in knowing Christ.

GOING DEEPER

1. Read Proverbs 3:5-6. How do these verses apply to coaching?
2. Second Peter 1:3 teaches that Jesus provides "all things that pertain to life and godliness." How does this apply to coaching?

--- LESSON 5 ---

A LEADER SACRIFICES FOR OTHERS

"Greater love has no one than this, that someone lay down his life for his friends."

John 15:13

Wake Forest University baseball coach Tom Walter, "took one for the team" when he donated his kidney to freshman outfielder Kevin Jordan. "I feel I was meant to be here with Kevin," said 42-year-old Walter, whose players call him "Walt." "I don't consider myself a hero. It's just doing the right thing." During the winter of 2010, Jordan's health began to rapidly decline. Two days before he had enrolled at Wake Forest for the fall semester, doctors told Jordan he needed a kidney transplant as soon as possible. Jordan completed the first semester of school while receiving dialysis. While doctors discussed Jordan's treatment and prognosis with Walter and a trainer, "our mouths were hanging open," said Walter. "We couldn't believe what he had endured. I made the decision immediately that if I could help, I would." After Jordan's mother and brother were not found to be good donor matches, Walter was tested. Walter learned he was a match. When he told his team a week ago that he'd be donating his kidney, the players gave him an enthusiastic round of applause.

1. What are some of the sacrifices a coach makes?
2. What are the most important sacrifices a coach makes?

WORKOUT

ROMANS 5:6-11

CONTEXT

The Apostle Paul is building on his argument that peace with God comes through faith in Jesus Christ. He traces peace with God all the way back to Abraham in Romans 4. It has always been about faith in the Messiah and always will be. Here in Romans 5, Paul explains that one of the most miraculous things about the sacrifice of Christ is that it was for His enemies.

EXPLORE THE MEANING

1. What stands out to you in this passage?
2. What does it mean that "Christ died for the ungodly"?

MAN'S WAY OR GOD'S WAY?

What motivates you to sacrifice time and energy for your athletes? Maybe it's a desire to help your athletes, a sense of duty, and/or the enjoyment of teaching? There are many reasons a coach might sacrifice for his team. For the Christian coach, the primary reason must be love. It is the greatest and most consistent motivating power in sports. Everything God has done for the believer, including Christ's death for man's sin, is based on love. No one has ever given so much for a people so unworthy. It is not even that people were simply bad; they were full-blown enemies. Yet, Christ died for His people and conquered death so they may have life.

GOING DEEPER

1. Christian coaching is to be motivated by a threefold love: Christ's love for us, our love for Christ and love for others. Discuss how this applies to your coaching.
2. How does Jesus' death and resurrection impact your life?

--- LESSON 6 ---

A LEADER IS CONFIDENT

"But thanks be to God, who always leads us in triumph in Christ."

2 Corinthians 2:14

During the majority of his quarterback career with the Huskers, the late Brook Berringer spent his time as a backup to 1995 All-American Tommie Frazier, but he chose not to let it bother him. Brook's opportunity to start came during Nebraska's '94 championship run when Frazier was sidelined with a blood clot behind his right knee. Brook started, and his team won the final seven games. But in 1995 with Frazier healthy, he found himself again on the sideline. And though Berringer possessed the ability to start almost anywhere else in the country, he never publicly complained about it. He was a team player. "He handled a tough situation as well as and with about as much dignity as anybody ever could. As coaches, we have tried to help our players remain confident regardless of their circumstances. It's not possible to be an effective leader and be pessimistic." said Head Coach Tom Osborne. For Brook, his source of confidence and contentment was his faith in Jesus Christ. "When I have something more specific to focus on, like my faith and my desire to grow in that faith, it brings everything into focus," said Brook.

1. How do most players usually respond when being demoted?
2. What has been your experience coaching a confident athlete like Brook? How did that impact your team?

WORKOUT
ROMANS 8:28-30

CONTEXT

The book of Romans is an incredible letter written by the Apostle Paul to the members of the church in Rome. His main reason for writing the letter was to teach the great truths of the Gospel of grace. Here in Romans 8, Paul is teaching that our future glory awaits believers and in light of this great hope, we should be encouraged and motivated to handle all the sufferings that life throws our way.

EXPLORE THE MEANING

1. What stands out to you in this passage?
2. Why does Paul link our confidence to our future glory?

MAN'S WAY OR GOD'S WAY?

Most athletes and coaches know that personal confidence is crucial to keep a team going. However, finding the right balance is not always easy. In fact, many individuals and teams are either over-confident or lack confidence. When confidence is based on our abilities or circumstances, there will always be a lack of consistency. From God's perspective, we can have confidence that He will accomplish His purposes in us because He loves us and has chosen to conform us to the image of His Son. It is in this reality that we can have confidence in any and every trial.

GOING DEEPER

1. Confidence is rooted in Gospel truth. How can you communicate this truth to others?
2. How does Romans 8:28-30 bring perspective to your team's wins and loses?

---- LESSON 7 ----

A LEADER IS TRUTHFUL

"Rather, speaking the truth in love, we are to grow up in every way into him who is the head, into Christ,"

Ephesians 4:15

Political correctness has complicated our lives, not to mention made coaching more difficult. Many of us have trouble saying what we really mean and meaning what we really say! We are so afraid of hurting someone's feelings, we back away from confrontation which would clarify issues, solve problems, and heal relationships. Mike Krzyzewski is an outstanding basketball coach at Duke University. He spoke of truthfulness in his book *A Season Is a Lifetime:* "When your life span is only eight short months, you're always aware of the pressures of time. There is simply no time to waste. We can't always take the nice, polite way of saying things to each other; we need to communicate in ways that are more direct than most people are used to. We can only do this if we learn to trust each other and to understand that we're not trying to hurt each other with our words, even when to someone outside our team they might seem destructive. I tell our players we can always deal with the truth; don't lie or cheat yourself or others. Being straightforward gets everyone on the same page quickly. Honesty helps develop in our individual and team character a strong sense of integrity."

1. Why can it be difficult for coaches to be truthful?
2. What types of issues are made more complicated by telling the truth?

WORKOUT

EPHESIANS 4:17-25

CONTEXT

The Bible continually uses the phrase "walk" as a way of describing one's life. In Ephesians 4, Paul calls Christians to walk in a manner worthy of their calling. They are to put off their old life and put on the new self. One of the first characteristics of this new life is truthfulness.

EXPLORE THE MEANING

1. What stood out to you in this passage?

2. What does it mean for a coach to put off the old self?

3. Discuss how Christians are different from the world in this passage.

MAN'S WAY OR GOD'S WAY?

In recent years, there have been too many examples of coaches who have not been truthful when dealing with their athletes and fans. Many coaches will avoid being truthful to protect themselves and their programs. However, the Apostle Paul commands all believers to put away falsehood...but he doesn't stop there, he adds: "let each one of you speak truth with his neighbor." This is helpful language, showing that we must not only cast off sinful habits but put on godly ones.

GOING DEEPER

1. What does truthfulness to your athletes look like?
2. How has the truth of the Gospel changed your life? How different do you look now?

---- LESSON 8 ----

A LEADER IS POISED

"And Jesus grew in wisdom and stature, and in favor with God and men."

Luke 2:52

Poise means "balance" or "stability," also "ease and dignity of manner." Here are two stories of coaches who believed poise was one of the most important traits of a successful athlete.

John Wooden often preached poise to his players. He said, "Self-control in little things leads to control of bigger things. For example, the reason I prohibited profanity during practices was because it was usually caused by frustration or anger. I felt that a player who couldn't control his language when he got upset during a scrimmage would be more likely to lose control in more damaging ways during the heat of a competition." During the 2006 volleyball season, John Cook's Nebraska volleyball team overcame a two game deficit in the regional finals. The media and fans wondered what Coach Cook told his players in the locker room during the break. He said, "Our team showed great poise coming back to win the Final Four. With so much on the line, we won the final three games and the match. That team was a great example of poise as they were able to handle the pressure because many of our players relied on the Lord so they were less anxious about their performances."

1. How does a coach's poise impact his athletes?
2. When have you seen poise determine the outcome

WORKOUT

LUKE 20:1-8

CONTEXT

Luke 20 includes a series of carefully coordinated attacks on Christ by the Jewish leaders who designed their questions to entrap Him. These leaders included the chief priests, scribes, and elders—key representatives of the elite Sanhedrin. These men were from a large council in Jerusalem, consisting of seventy-one prominent religious leaders, collectively known as the Sanhedrin. They had ultimate authority over Israel in all religious and spiritual matters and even Caesar recognized this authority in some civil affairs. Luke contrasts their authority with Jesus Christ, who has supreme authority over all things.

EXPLORE THE MEANING

1. What stood out to you in this passage?
2. How were the Pharisees trying to trap Jesus with their question in Luke 20:2? How did Jesus demonstrate poise?

MAN'S WAY OR GOD'S WAY?

True poise is possible for anyone who relies on God's strength and spirit. J.I. Packer wrote, "If your eyes are filled with light and working properly, your body will be able to move easily and safely. If you can't see clearly, you will lack physical ease and poise. Similarly, if your heart is possessed by what this world and this life offers, you will not be able to see spiritual issues clearly, and when you read the Bible, its full meaning will escape you."

GOING DEEPER

1. How did Jesus' poise help Him respond to their question?
2. What can you apply from this lesson to your coaching?

---- *LESSON 9* ----

A LEADER IS PURPOSEFUL

"So whatever you eat or drink, or whatever you do, do all to the glory of God."

1 Corinthians 10:31

UTEP Coach Don Haskins had a specific purpose with his starting line-up in the 1966 NCAA National Championship basketball game in College Park, Maryland. Facing the top-ranked University of Kentucky in the championship game, Haskins made history by starting five African-American players for the first time in a championship game against Kentucky's all-white squad, coached by Adolph Rupp. The UTEP Miners beat Kentucky 72-65, winning the tournament and finishing the year with a 28-1 record. While wanting to place his best players on the court, he also knew there was another purpose which would motivate his players to win the game. His opponent had won five national championships and still refused to recruit black players. Hours before the game, Haskins told his team that he heard Coach Rupp vow that "no five blacks are going to beat Kentucky." Were the Miners motivated?

"Kentucky was playing for a commemorative wristwatch and the right to say they were national champions," said Harry Flournoy, who averaged 8.3 points and 10.7 rebounds for UTEP. "We were out to prove that it didn't matter what color a person's skin was."

1. What are reasons that motivate coaches and athletes?
2. What are the problems with some of these reasons?

WORKOUT

JOHN 12:36,43

CONTEXT

John lists two causes for Israel's unbelief, one divine and the other human. They illustrate the interface between divine sovereignty and human responsibility. The personal or human choice involved in rejecting Jesus Christ is illustrated by the rulers who believed in Him. They were not confessing Him because they feared rejection from the Pharisees; therefore their faith was inadequate. They wanted the approval or glory of man more than the glory that comes from God.

EXPLORE THE MEANING

1. What stood out to you in the passage?
2. Is there anyone or group that coaches often fear? Why?

MAN'S WAY OR GOD'S WAY??

Many coaches find purpose in their career through bringing glory to themselves, their schools, or the community. Others like Don Haskins find purpose by helping to integrate college basketball or win a national championship. While these might be noble reasons to coach, nothing compares to coaching for the glory of God. Jesus is the definition of a person having purpose. Luke records that He set his face toward Jerusalem (9:51) even though it meant that He would die. Jesus' sole purpose was to please His Heavenly Father.

GOING DEEPER

1. What are examples of coaches seeking their own glory?
2. How can a coach reflect and amplify God's glory to others?

---- *LESSON 10* ----

A LEADER IS SELF-CONTROLLED

"A man without self-control is like a city broken into and left without walls."

Proverbs 25:28

Jim Harbaugh charged across the field, lifting his shirt to expose his belly to attempt a chest bump. He extended his right hand to Jim Schwartz for a shake and slapped him on the back with his left hand. Schwartz didn't like what was done or said—claiming he heard an expletive—and went charging after Harbaugh. What an emotional scene following a hyped-up, high-profile meeting of turnaround teams in San Francisco's 25-19 victory over Detroit! After the incident, both coaches offered apologies for their actions. "That is totally on me," Harbaugh said. "I shook his hand too hard. I really went in, and it was a strong, kind of a slap-grab handshake."

"It's unfortunate," Schwartz told reporters. "The game is played by the players on the field. We certainly don't want things like that to occur. There are competitive people in the league, and I think we need to do a better job of just leaving it to the players on the field."

1. Describe a game or practice when you lost self-control. What resulted from your loss of control?
2. Describe a time when you displayed tremendous self-control. What happened in this situation?

WORKOUT
1 CORINTHIANS 10:6-13

CONTEXT

One of the main ways to fall into temptation and sin is to become overconfident. Many of the Corinthian believers felt perfectly secure in their Christian lives, with a mindset that they had arrived. In this passage, Paul reminds them to be careful not to become overconfident. Paul used Israel as an example of the dangers of overconfidence. Earlier in 1 Corinthians 10, he uses their forty–year wandering between Egypt and Canaan as an example of the pitfalls of overconfidence.

EXPLORE THE MEANING

1. What stood out to you in this passage?
2. What would be an example of a coach who becomes overconfident in his spiritual walk? What is the result?

MAN'S WAY OR GOD'S WAY?

Even unbelieving coaches view self-control as a necessary part of sports to be successful. In Jesus' day, the word translated "self-control" was used to describe athletes. Those who were successful abstained from certain activities for the sake of disciplined training exercises. For the Christian coach, self-control is about pleasing God so that it's possible to control his desires rather than allowing them to control him.

GOING DEEPER

1. What are some practices that have helped you develop self-control?
2. How can pursuing discipline in some of these areas carry over to the spiritual areas?

---- LESSON 11 ----

A LEADER IS ENERGETIC

"I can do all this through him who gives me strength."

Philippians 4:13

At the age of 38, Dick Vermeil had the college football world in the palm of his hand. The young coach from the West went east and became the head coach of the Philadelphia Eagles in 1976. Five years later, his Eagles were in their first Super Bowl. He was named the NFL's Coach of the Year in 1980, and led the Eagles into Super Bowl XV after defeating the Dallas Cowboys for the NFC championship. He retired for the first time after the 1982 season citing "severe burnout."

Fatigue has afflicted many coaches, including Urban Meyer. He made the surprising decision in 2010 to step down as head football coach at Florida after a very successful career, citing the overall grind of coaching and the toll it took on his personal life. The life of a coach is a unique career experience when compared to more traditional jobs—especially with high profile coaching positions. Coaches like Meyer enjoy the benefits that come with coaching, but also struggle to find time in their lives to spend with families because of being "on the job" 24/7 during their seasons.

1. What wears you down during your season?
2. What advice regarding priorities would you give to a coach just beginning his/her career?

WORKOUT

PHILIPPIANS 4:10-19

CONTEXT

The Apostle Paul teaches his readers the secret of contentment here in Philippians. Contentment relates directly to how much energy or weariness we feel in adversity. The Bible has a lot to say about being content. Paul said in 1 Timothy 6:6, "Godliness with contentment is great gain." Most people seek contentment and assume that contentment is the absence of all problems. That's not the true meaning of contentment. If it was, no one would ever have it because you can't be completely free from problems. True contentment is being able to be satisfied and content in the midst of any problem. That's the kind of contentment God offers through Christ.

EXPLORE THE MEANING

1. What stood out to you in the passage?
2. How does contentment relate to spiritual burnout?

MAN'S WAY OR GOD'S WAY?

Some coaches look forward to their off-season to refresh themselves and recover from the pressures of coaching. While it's important to get the necessary rest, the Christian coach knows his true rest and satisfaction is related to living life through understanding the providence of God. Resting in God's promise brings satisfaction as we look forward to our eternal home in Heaven.

GOING DEEPER

1. What is the connection between Christ providing the strength to live the Christian life and contentment?
2. How can a coach be content without becoming complacent?

---- LESSON 12 ----

A LEADER IS DETERMINED

*"I have fought the good fight,
I have finished the race, I have kept the faith."*

2 Timothy 4:7

Prior to the 2011-12 season, 59-year old basketball coach Pat Summitt had won eight NCAA National Championships and 1,071 games. With her famous icy glare, she recently announced she would continue coaching as she stares down early-onset Alzheimer's Disease. As Summitt entered her 39th season as coach at the University of Tennessee, she was diagnosed in May 2011 and told the world. Reaction was shock giving way to dismay, tempered by admiration for her fighting spirit.

Summitt wrote an open letter to the university community. "I plan to continue to be your coach," she wrote. "Obviously, I realize I may have some limitations with this condition since there will be some good days and some bad days. For that reason, I will be relying on my outstanding coaching staff like never before." That is perhaps the only known quantity in all this. What lies ahead is mostly about the unknown—how her condition might progress, how stress might affect it, and how her players might react to all the attention focused on the health of their coach.

1. Do you think coaches are more determined than others? Why or why not?

WORKOUT
PHILIPPIANS 3:12-16

CONTEXT

The Apostle Paul uses the analogy of a runner to describe the Christian's spiritual growth. Since believers have not reached their goal of Christlikeness, they must continue to pursue it like the runner in a race. This goal of becoming like Christ is repeated many times in the Bible and is clear from passages like Romans 8:29, "For those He foreknew He also predestined to be conformed to the image of His Son, in order that He might be the firstborn among many brothers."

EXPLORE THE MEANING

1. What is the upward call of God?
2. How is Paul determined to meet this goal?

MAN'S WAY OR GOD'S WAY?

Many coaches pursue goals that will only disappoint and frustrate them throughout their careers, but the Christian coach should have a much greater goal. Just as the Apostle Paul was still striving with the purpose of being Christlike, how much more should we be striving to be like our Savior? Christlikeness should be our goal in all we do. We should be determined to obtain it and press forward at all times. Paul was determined to be obedient so as to not disqualify himself from the prize. He had a goal and was determined to meet it.

GOING DEEPER

1. What are the common goals many coaches spend their lives pursuing? How can these be disappointing?
2. Are most coaches determined to become more like Christ? Why or why not?

www.ingramcontent.com/pod-product-compliance
Lightning Source LLC
Chambersburg PA
CBHW052204110526
44591CB00012B/2072